One of the underlying principles that informs the theory and practice of permaculture is that it is the connections that develop and flourish between the elements of an ecosystem on which the strength, productivity and durability of that system depends. Whether it be the connections that form between people as they cooperate and share their skills, the sense of a bond that grows up between a gardener and their garden as it develops over time and provides a yield, or the way that animals develop intricate associations within an ecosystem to ensure its continued survival, connections are everything.

Such links, bonds and relationships can also be observed between plant species. Indeed, you can see it everywhere in natural environments that haven't been modified and distorted by human interference, which too often leads to environments such as the vast swathes of monocultures in industrial agriculture, or the almost desert-like uniformity that develops in vegetation that is exposed to overgrazing by livestock. Plants in the wilderness, on the whole, work together to

get your free permaculture checklist now @
regenerative.com/book-checklist

Regenerative Leadership Institute
create a meaningful life doing what you love

create a harmonious, balanced ecosystem. Of course, as with many arrangements of individuals there are some that have a more pernicious effect (such as vines that strangle trees or weeds that crowd out other species with their fast-growing, nutrient-hungry development), but on the whole plants create and sustain connections that enable them to live alongside one another and even to reap benefits because of that proximity. Plants also develop relationships with all types of animals, and many of these relationships are essential to the health of the plant, its continued survival and its ability to propagate itself.

Look at a natural temperate forest, for example. Such an ecosystem is replete with many different species of plant, from the tallest trees to the smallest flowers, through shrubs, understorey trees and plants, ground covers, brambles, lichens, mosses and ferns. All co-exist side-by-side, evolving over time as an inter-related collection of specimens, each with a different relationship to one another. Many will also have intricate relationships with a variety of animals that frequent the forest – from organisms that live in the soil (ranging from bacteria and nematodes to worms and moles) or inhabit the plant itself (from insect larvae to owls and woodpeckers) to migrant animals that visit for, say, just one season when the plant is most laden with fruit or nuts. And, in turn, these animals develop connections between different species within the ecosystem, not only in terms of a food chain, but also, for instance, by relying on one another to give warnings of danger or cover from potential attack by flocking together in the case of various bird species.

In fact, not only could you say that a forest – which refers not only the plants, but also to the animals and the soil – acts something like an organism, with each constituent part performing a function, or occupying a niche, that contributes to the whole, it can even be said that every individual tree – such are the number of connections with surrounding plants that it has – can be considered the center of an ecosystem or "organism" in its own right.

And it is the benefits that certain relationships between plants bring to one another that we seek to emulate as permaculture gardeners when we plan our planting patterns and arrangements. Among the best ways to harness these positive attributes are the techniques of companion planting, guild planting and succession planting.

The Benefits of Companion Planting

So when it comes to creating connections between plant species – and harnessing the relationships that certain plants and animals have with one another – on a permaculture property, the simplest method is what is known as companion planting. Essentially this refers to growing two species of plants next to one another because of the benefits that doing so brings to each one.

get your free permaculture checklist now @
regenerative.com/book-checklist

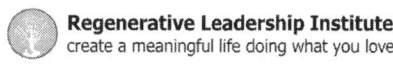
Regenerative Leadership Institute
create a meaningful life doing what you love

So what exactly are these benefits? Well, the first and perhaps most important is that by utilizing the beneficial symbiotic relationship between the plant species you help them to thrive, to grow more robustly and to provide the gardener with more yield. By planting species together that aid one another in some aspect of their life processes, you improve the chances of both plants maturing and setting a crop that is healthy, full and vibrant.

Furthermore, by planning your planting arrangements so that you use conglomerations of different species – these arrangements don't have to just be comprised of two species, you can create planting configurations that involve several species all working together, something that will be discussed later – you increase the variety of plants on your site. Rather than garden beds filled with a single crop, you have beds that have two, three or more different plant species. This increases the property's biodiversity, which itself has several tangible benefits, from making for a more resilient ecosystem that can better

stand up should it be exposed, for example, to extreme climatic events or an adverse soil pathogen, to providing a more aesthetically pleasing site, one that is full of the abundance and variety of nature as opposed to just a few plant species. This variety will have the knock-on effect of attracting a larger array of insects and wild animals to your site, which can be beneficial in terms of pollination, pest control and propagation, as well as making the garden a more fascinating place to be.

Utilizing companion planting will also help to maintain a good balance of nutrients in the soil (which, again, helps productivity as it ensures that each species has access to the combination of elements it needs for healthy growth). Different plants have different nutritional needs. Berry fruits, for instance, require higher levels of potassium in order to set their crops than, say, nut trees do. Other species are particularly nitrogen-hungry, while others require more phosphorous in order to thrive. By combining species with different nutritional needs in the same bed the permaculture gardener can help each satisfy their requirements, and often the arrangements used in companion planting will use one plant to actively provide more of the nutrients required to the soil so the other plant can use them.

The benefits that plants located in proximity to one another can provide extend to the soil itself. By including species that send down deep roots, you help improve the soil structure for all the species in the garden bed, particularly those with shallower roots. The augmented soil structure helps those shallower-lying plants to get a more robust grip on the land, and allows them to more easily access the soil moisture and nutrients they need to survive and thrive. The deeper-rooting plants also help to bring up water and nutritional elements from further down in the soil profile to the surface where other plants can use them, adding to the beneficial growing conditions in the topsoil.

Above the soil surface, the benefits of companion planting continue. By incorporating a variety of plant species into your garden bed designs,

get your free permaculture checklist now @
regenerative.com/book-checklist

Regenerative Leadership Institute
create a meaningful life doing what you love

you can provide specimens with positive enhancements due to the physical structure of their neighbors. For instance, taller plants located next to lower lying varieties can offer protection from wind, rain and excessive solar radiation. This can be particularly important for juvenile seedlings that are trying to establish themselves in a bed. They are much more susceptible to the detrimental effects of extreme weather conditions, and companion planting can offer them a kind of haven in which to mature. This effect is sometimes known as "nursing". Such positive impacts can also be provided if the permaculture gardener makes "stacking" part of the companion planting design. Like the forest ecosystem mentioned previously, companion planting designs can involve different levels of plants, featuring species that grow to differing heights. Not only does this mean that more plants can be placed into a single bed – increasing the biomass and, thus, the yield of your site – but it also means that different plant species receive the conditions they need to grow well at least in part from their neighbors. Tall plants that require a lot of exposure to sunlight aid those lower down in the

stacking system that need a greater degree of shade. Those lower lying plants may, in turn, cover the ground, preventing excessive moisture evaporation and retaining water in the soil that the taller plants can then access with their roots. Furthermore, some companion plants can actually provide the structure on which their neighbors grow, serving as a kind of natural trellis, if you like. Vines growing on trees are an example of this kind of relationship. In return, the vines may protect the tree from certain pests or exposure to wind.

The benefits of companion planting are also evident even after you harvest your crops. Certain arrangements of plant species will actually help improve the flavor of crops simply by growing next to one another. For example, planting herbs like chives next to strawberries will help to enhance the "strawberry-ness" of the fruit once it is ripe for picking. It seems that not only does the strong scent of the chives mask the aroma of the strawberries, making their detection by slugs and other pests less likely and protecting your crop, but the fact that chives help to accumulate potassium and calcium in the soil surrounding them also plays a part in making the fruit more delicious. The chives help supply potassium to the fruit both when growing and, as a secondary benefit, when they are cut back and left as mulch after flowering.

Other pairings of companion plants actually go well together in the kitchen, their complimentary nature extending from the garden bed to the plate. As well as providing harmonious flavours for your tastebuds, this has the added benefit of placing plants that you would want to harvest together (in order to make a dish) right next door to one another, making picking the harvest easier and saving you the energy of walking to different beds to get the plants you want.

Connections between plants and animals

This reciprocity is an example of the binary or symbiotic nature that many companion planting arrangements have, and such a connection is often observed in the relationships that plant species develop with animals. Another positive influence of companion planting is that is can serve to attract beneficial organisms to your site, deter unwanted visitors, and help control pest species – all with the express purpose of helping your crop plants to flourish.

One way that companion planting can affect animal impacts on your site is by using one species of plant to camouflage another that is often prey to browsers, either physically by growing over it so that it is less easily spotted, or by using scent or confusing visual signals to stop microorganisms like insects from distinguishing their target from the other plants around it. The permaculture gardener can also use some types of plants as a distraction for animals, drawing them away from

get your free permaculture checklist now @
regenerative.com/book-checklist

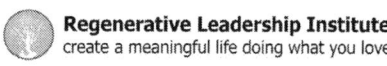

a more vulnerable species – with the companion acting as a kind of decoy. In more extreme cases, the permaculture gardener may resort to planting a species next to a more valuable, vulnerable one that is under attack from a pest insect in order to lure the pests away, essentially sacrificing the one plant species to protect the crop of the other.

Besides deterring animals, companion planting can also be used to attract them. If, for instance, one species of plant is often under attack from a certain kind of insect, you may be able to plant a second species nearby that attracts insects that prey on the pests, helping to keep their numbers down and protect your crops from too much damage (while avoiding any input of insecticides). This can also work on a larger scale by, for example, planting prickly or thorny species of plant on the outside border of species prone to grazing by wild deer or rabbits. They then act as a barrier to prevent the animals eating your crops. You can also plant certain species – particularly ones that have bright, scented flowers – next to less conspicuous specimens in order to attract a greater number of pollinating insects which will, in turn, find their way to neighboring plants and so help propagate them.

Companion examples

Having explored the many benefits of companion planting, let's have a look at some practical examples of popular species that are compatible with one another – as well as some of the combinations of plants to avoid in your permaculture planting plan – in order to maximize the growing potential of your property.

Fruit companions

Let's start with some of the common fruits that permaculture gardeners may grow. Blackberries, for instance, are themselves useful companion plants to many vegetable species, as the thorny brambles that they grow on make excellent deterrents for deer, rabbits and other wild grazers. However, the blackberry itself is prone to depletion by birds, so if you value your blackberry crop highly – either as a product to sell or because it is one of your favorite fruits to eat – consider planting chokeberries or elderberries nearby as these can act as decoys for birds, luring them away from the blackberries. You should avoid planting blackberries in close proximity to raspberries as their similar chemical make-up means that they will be competing with each other for soil nutrients, which is likely to result in one or both crops underperforming. They also prefer different acidity levels in the soil, so providing each with the ideal conditions when near each other would prove very difficult to achieve.

Raspberries themselves should also be kept at a distance from potatoes, as if they are placed in proximity it increases the risk of the potatoes being attacked by blight. Companion planting with tansy flowers helps protect raspberries from many of the insect species that would attack them, such as the Japanese beetle, as well as adding

potassium to the soil, which the raspberries benefit from having access to in terms of setting their fruit crop.

Strawberries, being a low-lying crop, can serve as living mulch for many other plant species, suppressing weeds and conserving soil moisture. In turn, strawberry plants benefit from planting in conjunction with species that protect them from insects, as they are vulnerable to attack from a wide range of microorganisms. Flowering herbs planted nearby help attract beneficial insects that predate pests, with borage a particularly useful companion. Its flowers are also very efficient in attracting bees, which in turn help to pollinate the strawberry plants. Catnip and rue are other herbs that help strawberries thrive; in their case by repelling potentially damaging insects such as aphids and cabbage loppers. Onion and garlic planted alongside can also deter pests with their pungent aromas (which don't, however, taint the taste or smell of the strawberry crop), while marigolds make a good companion for strawberries if your soil is prone to nematodes.

Grapes will do best if planted as companions to legumes, a family of plants that add nitrogen to the soil. The fruit need the nitrogen to set a healthy, abundant crop. While most grapes are grown on trellises, if you have an elm or a mulberry tree on your property, this can provide a good support for a grape vine and won't be damaged by the vines.

Turning to tree fruits, apples do well when planted alongside species such as alliums that help suppress grass and weeds that would compete with the trees for water and soil moisture. Apricots, meanwhile, can be offered defence by establishing a connection with basil and garlic, which deter pests from damaging the apricot tree via their aromas – in the former's case repelling insects, in the latter's moles and aphids. Avoid planting potatoes or tomatoes near apricot trees, as these species make the transference of molds and fungi to the fruit tree more likely, stunting growth and diminishing crops. The advice for companion planting for apricots also applies to peaches and nectarines.

Citrus fruits are heavy nitrogen feeders; so making them companion plants to leguminous vegetables which fix nitrogen in the soil is a good idea. Dill and thyme are good flowering herb companions to attract insects that will pollinate the citrus tree, while yarrow is a good companion as it attracts ladybugs which feed on the aphids that can prove damaging to the citrus plant. Parsley is also a defender of citrus trees, by attracting parasitic wasps, which predate the caterpillars that can attack the tree.

Pears, too, like a lot of nitrogen in the soil, so companion planting with legumes is a good strategy. Eggplant and morning glory planted nearby will help by attracting ladybugs and other beneficial insects that eat aphids, which suck out sap from the pear tree, reducing the flow of nutrients to the leaves and fruits. Borage helps attract bees that pollinate the pear tree while also adding calcium and potassium to the soil, and alliums like chives and leeks will help – as they do with most fruit trees – by suppressing competing grasses and weeds and repelling slugs and aphids.

get your free permaculture checklist now @
regenerative.com/book-checklist

Regenerative Leadership Institute
create a meaningful life doing what you love

When it comes to that most vegetable-like of fruits, the tomato does well in proximity to basil – unsurprisingly perhaps when you consider their complimentary tastes in the kitchen. The basil helps to protect the tomatoes from aphids and spider mites, and attracts bees that help pollinate the fruits. It also actually improves the "tomato-y" flavor of the fruit. Chives and garlic also help protect tomatoes from insect attack. Tomatoes combine well with asparagus – as the fruits protect the vegetable from the damaging asparagus beetle – and gooseberries, which deter several different types of pest insects. Avoid planting tomatoes near potatoes (as they make the potatoes more likely to contract blight), apricot trees (as they inhibit growth), or corn (as they can attract pests that will eat the corn).

Vegetable companions

Moving on to actual vegetables, the allium family – which, alongside chives and leeks, includes onions, garlic and shallots – does particularly well when planted in proximity to carrots (while, in turn, they serve to repel the damaging carrot fly from visiting their neighbors). Salad greens like lettuce planted with alliums are afforded protection by the alliums' ability to deter slugs. Beans and peas should not be planted near alliums, however, as they tend to attract insect species that feed on the allium plants.

Beans themselves, being leguminous, are good companions for a whole host of plant species that require high levels of nitrogen in the soil, particularly fruit trees and members of the Brassica family. The beans benefit from close connections to potatoes and marigolds, as these plant species repel insect pests that could damage the beans. Because beans are relatively light feeders when it comes to soil nutrients, they can be good companions for those species that require a lot from the soil, such as cucumbers and cabbages.

Beans are, in fact, part of one of the most well known forms of companion planting strategy. The "Three Sisters" is thought to have originated among Native American tribes more than six centuries ago, and it remains an effective way of combining three crops – beans, corn and squash. Each of the three parts of this trio brings effects that help them all thrive, while benefiting in turn from the advantages given by proximity to their "siblings". So, the corn provides support for the beans to grow on. The beans, for their part, help "fix" nitrogen in the soil, which benefits all three members of the sorority, while the lower lying squash provides a living mulch that prevents the evaporation of soil moisture and keeps weeds out (and the prickly leaves of the squash also deter racoons and other wild animals that would otherwise graze on the corn and beans). This is an early example of a guild – something we will explore later in this book.

For broccoli and other members of the Brassica family – which includes cauliflower, kale, collards and Brussels sprouts – companion planting with fragrant herbs is a good idea. Species such as sage, rosemary,

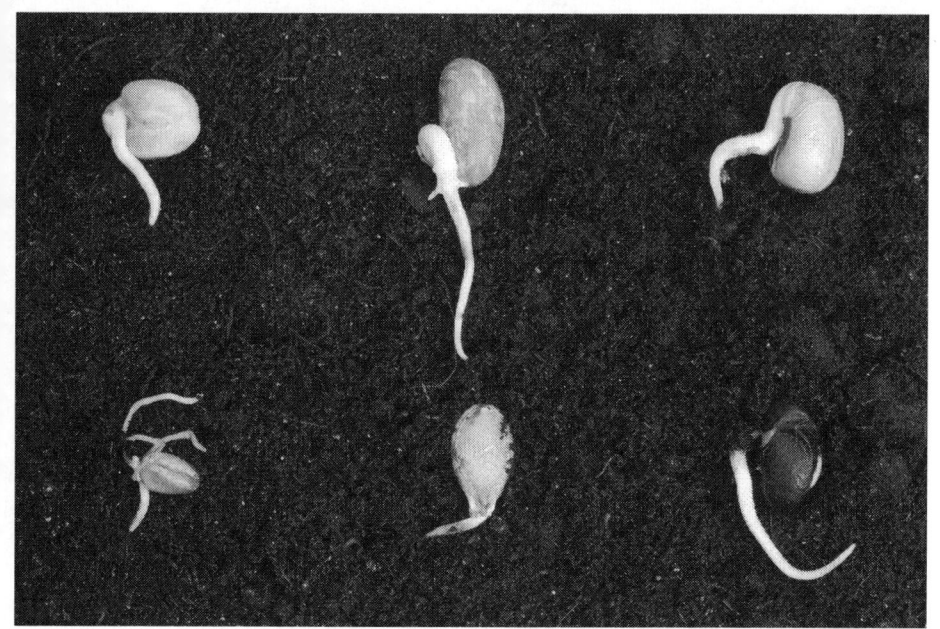

basil and mint placed nearby help to deter insects that would feed on the Brassica crop. All Brassicas are relatively heavy feeders when it comes to soil nutrients – particularly of calcium – so despite being a family, it makes sense not to group all your Brassica plants together in your garden beds, as they will compete for the same nutrients. For the same reason, avoid planting next to other heavy feeders such as sweet corn, pumpkin and asparagus – light feeders like nasturtiums and beets make good neighbors as they leave the lion's share of calcium available for the Brassicas.

Speaking of beets, they benefit from being teamed with garlic, the aroma of which puts off potential soil-dwelling pests like root maggots, Japanese beetles and coddling moths that could attack the beet below the surface of the soil where the gardener can't see the damage often until its too late to save the plant. Beets also grow well in combination with bush beans such as soybeans and butter beans, but are inhibited in their growth if placed next to pole beans. Mint is an ideal companion

for beets, however, as not only does the aroma deter moths, aphids and even some rodents from attacking the beets, it tastes great when combined with the beets in your kitchen – planting them together saves energy when harvesting as you can collect them at the same time.

As mentioned previously, carrots in concert with alliums provides benefits to both parties – in the case of the former by repelling the potentially damaging carrot fly, which lays its eggs around juvenile carrot plants so that the larvae can feed on the root as soon as they hatch. (Carrot fly can also affect parsnips and celery, so it is a good strategy to combine them with alliums in your planting plan as well.)

Cucumber is a plant that likes some shade so can be combined with fruit trees as an understorey plant, while locating next to radishes helps to protect the crop from cucumber beetles. Avoid placing cucumbers next to potatoes, as this seems to make the potatoes more susceptible to blight.

Another popular salad vegetable, lettuce does well next to onions as the onion fixes lots of nitrogen to the soil, which the lettuce feeds heavily on to set its crop. The aroma of the onion is also adept at deterring rabbits that would seek to make of meal of your lettuce leaves. Onions themselves do well alongside many different plants, including the Brassica family, tomatoes, lettuce, beets and strawberries. However, they are best keep apart from beans and peas as these compete for the same proportions of soil nutrients.

Pumpkins can replace squash in the Three Sisters trio of companions, but should be kept separate from potatoes as they inhibit one another's growth. Sweet peppers, meanwhile, combine well with basil – and they go well together in the kitchen as well – and gain protection from okra when the latter is planted as a windbreak (because the pepper plants are comparatively brittle and can be easily damaged if your property is exposed to strong winds). Spinach and eggplant do well when close to one another, accessing

get your free permaculture checklist now @
regenerative.com/book-checklist

Regenerative Leadership Institute
create a meaningful life doing what you love

complimentary proportions of soil nutrients. Spinach is also a good companion for strawberries.

Herb companions

As we've seen throughout the vegetable and fruit sections, herbs often make excellent companions for a wide variety of other plant species, primarily either through deterring pests or attracting pollinators to the permaculture property. But let's explore some of the companions that help the herbs themselves to grow to their potential.

Basil, for instance, is boosted not only by being in close proximity to tomatoes, but also to chamomile. Garlic, meanwhile, helps to protect it from grazers and provides another delightful flavor combination when used in conjunction in the kitchen. It is recommended that you don't plant basil next to rue, as this will inhibit the growth of both species. Rue itself, however, can prove useful at deterring Japanese beetles from raspberries when planted nearby, and is a good understorey plant for fruit trees as a weed-suppressing companion. Dill's growth is improved by connecting with cabbage, but does not do very well when located near to carrots or tomatoes. Mint will also do well near to cabbage, but likes tomatoes too. Peppermint, sage and rosemary all work as companions to cabbage as well.

Fennel is one of the most unpopular herbs when it comes to garden companions. Most other commonly cultivated species in a permaculture garden dislike being near to it, and it is particularly damaging to the growth of tomatoes and bush beans. This may make growing fennel in containers – as long as the containers are quite deep – the best option, particularly if you have limited space on your property and are determined to grow this particular herb. However you choose to grow it, keep fennel away from coriander for its own good, as coriander prevents the fennel from setting seeds. Coriander itself, however,

benefits from proximity to beans and peas; primarily for the nitrogen boost such species give to the surrounding soil.

Grain companions

Companion planting can also be a useful cultivation strategy in zones of your permaculture property that are further away from the house. Grain and other field crops can benefit from suitable neighboring species, which can help ensure their productivity, which is particularly important if you are growing such crops for the market or as essential winter fodder for your livestock.

The "Three Sisters" can be an example of this, aiding the cultivation of corn. Oats, meanwhile, do well when planted next to vetch. If you are growing wheat for harvest, a smattering a chamomile can aid growth, but must not exceed a ratio of around 1 to 100 as above this level it can prove detrimental. Plants to avoid planting near wheat include

cherry trees and sorghum, both of which will adversely affect yield, in the latter's case by poisoning the roots of the wheat. Sorghum should also be kept away from sesame for the same reason.

Other crop pairings that aid growth include cotton with alfalfa – with the latter helping to keep the cotton free of root rot – and flax and potatoes, with the flax serving to deter the potato beetle.

The parts of a guild

Guilds take the notion of companion planting – the positive interactions between plant species and the connections they make with animals – and steps it up a level. A guild is a planting arrangement that incorporates several different species of plant, each of which performs a function that has a positive impact upon the growing system as a whole, giving all the members of the guild the best conditions in which to survive

and thrive and, in turn, maximizing the potential for yield for the permaculture gardener.

So what are some of the roles that plants play within a guild? Well, one of the first ones to consider is that of a "feeder". These are the plant species that will, directly and indirectly, provide the gardener with food. They will range from fruit, vegetable and herb crops that are harvested from the table (which, as outlined above, are often grown together because not only do they provide benefits when in the soil near to one another, but also taste great together), to plants that provide forage for livestock (which will in turn give the gardener food products such as eggs, milk and meat) and flowers that provide pollen to bees that the gardener keeps to provide honey.

Other members of the guild will feed the soil, adding and fixing nutrients within the soil profile so that they and the plant specimens surrounding them have access to the chemical elements they need for robust growth and to set good crops. Some of the key "fixers" in a guild are those that increase the level of nitrogen in the soil. Nitrogen is, alongside water, the most essential element that plants need in order to perform their life processes, such as manufacturing chlorophyll for use in photosynthesis, and in synthesizing proteins. While an excessive amount of nitrogen in the soil can be detrimental to some plants – juvenile specimens, in particular, can be damaged if exposed to too much nitrogen – ensuring a good supply is something to aim for in your permaculture beds. Fortunately there are plants that increase nitrogen in the soil, lessening the need for soil additives and often giving you the secondary benefit of a crop yield. Chief among the nitrogen fixers are the legumes. In a prime example of a symbiotic relationship that can evolve between two different organisms, legumes provide a home to certain soil bacteria called Rhizobia on their root nodules. In return these bacteria transform nitrogen that is in the air that circulates through the soil (as long as the soil is well structured) into a form that the plants can take up via solution through their roots. While this relationship ensure that the legume has access to the nitrogen it needs, some of the chemical also becomes available to surrounding plants as well, boosting the guild as a whole. Legumes such as peas, beans and lentils will also provide a yield of edible crops for your kitchen, while other members of the family such as alfalfa and clover can be good sources of fodder for your livestock.

The other benefit of incorporating legumes into a guild is that once you have harvested the crop, the remaining plant parts can be cut back and left where they fall to act as a mulch for the rest of the guild; the nitrogen and other nutrients still contained within them returns to the soil via decomposition to further enhance living plants' growing conditions. This is also true of other members of the guild that shed their leaves. This "leaf litter" can provide valuable nutrients to the soil and, in turn, the plants growing in it. When leaves fall to the ground, the microorganisms in the soil get to work breaking them down, releasing the chemical elements they contain into the soil where it can

Want to Apply
Permaculture
ON YOUR PROPERTY NOW?

 Download your FREE Permaculture Property Checklists at
REGENERATIVE.COM/BOOK-CHECKLIST

www.regenerative.com

be accessed by plant roots. Traditional gardeners typically spend a lot of time raking up fallen leaves in an attempt to preserve some kind of aesthetic purity about their site, but what could be more beautiful to the eye than seeing a plant guild mimicking what happens in nature and making sure that nothing with potential energy goes to waste?

Other types of plant that enhance the soil for a guild include those that send down deep roots. These "diggers" serve a dual purpose. Firstly, their relative depth of root means that they can bring up moisture and nutrients from further down in the soil profile than their shallower lying cousins. These surface rooters can then access the elements when they are brought up to the topsoil. Secondly, their strong, extensive root systems help to improve the structure of the soil. This not only gives other plants a better chance of themselves establishing a robust root system (shallow rooting species especially need a good soil structure so that they can anchor themselves well even if their roots do not extend very far downwards), but also allows for the

effective percolation of moisture through the soil and the circulation of atmospheric gases, both of which are essential for all the plants in the guild to grow well. A subsidiary benefit is that deep rooting plants that improve the soil structure of the guild also give microorganisms and insects in the soil more room to manoeuvre, so to speak, allowing them to get on with the processes of decomposing organic matter. Indeed, some animals could be designated as "diggers", such as worms and moles, as they root through the soil, breaking it up and improving its structure, and so allowing plant roots to penetrate better – another example of a connection made between plants and animals.

There are also members of a guild that help maintain a healthy soil from above – by covering it. Ground cover crops help to protect the soil from erosion by rain and wind, as well as from compaction caused by exposure to either livestock or excessive solar radiation. They can also be beneficial in preventing evaporation of moisture from the soil and in stopping weeds from getting a foothold within the guild.

get your free permaculture checklist now @
regenerative.com/book-checklist

Regenerative Leadership Institute
create a meaningful life doing what you love

Nature abhors bare soil, and permaculture farmers follow nature's lead; instituting cover crops as part of a guild helps to keep bare soil to a minimum, and improves growing conditions for all members of the ecosystem.

Two other types of members of a guild have a more immediately obvious companion relationship: climbers and supporters. Some species of plant climb up structures in order to give themselves the support they need to grow (they typically have slender stems and branches and, hence, smaller crops – think of beans and passion fruit as examples). In a guild, other plants, particularly those with sturdy stems and thick branches, can provide this support. Obviously care must be taken that certain climbers do not overwhelm their supportive cousins, inhibiting their growth and development, but with the correct pairings, guilds can provide for this kind of support and negate the need for the gardener to institute fences or trellises for the climbers to cling too. Organising species in this way also helps

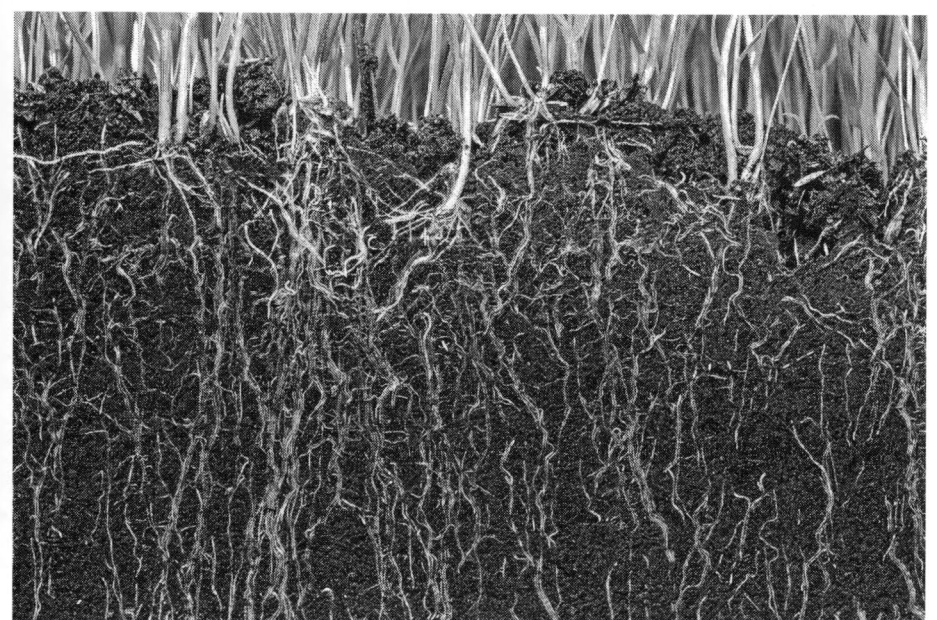

to maximize the growing potential of the guild, utilizing niches at different heights for different species to grow in, and increasing the biodiversity and biomass of the guild.

Plants can offer one another support in a guild in less obvious ways as well. Certain species can provide protection for others, in several ways. As mentioned previously, the permaculture gardener can locate plants species in proximity to one another to deter insect pests from attacking one of them, either by emitting an odor that the insects find unpleasant, confusing them with aromas, colors or shapes, or attracting other animals that predate the pests. Plants can also offer protection from larger animals by presenting an impenetrable barrier of thorns, or as well by utilizing smells that the animals seek to avoid. In a similar way, a plant-animal connection can also be useful, both in terms of livestock and wild creatures. For instance, allowing your ducks to periodically graze a guild will help to keep slug numbers down, which in turn will mean less damage to the plants in the guild, while providing suitable habitat for, say, insect-eating birds or lizards (typically by providing them with habitat that affords shelter from the eyes of their own predators) will help keep insect pest populations under control, again helping the plants to thrive.

Protection can also come in the form of plants offering others a defence against the elements. Taller plants are often utilized in a guild to provide shade for lower-lying or more vulnerable species, while denser plants can be used as windbreaks to ameliorate the effects of wind damage on less robust specimens.

Of course, it goes without saying that each plant species within a guild does not have to only perform a single function. Many can have several roles within the guild. Some species might be both rooters and supporters, for example, while others could aid soil structure while also offering protection to others from pest attack.

An example of a guild

To put all these various roles and functions of plants in a guild into perspective, let's look at an example. Now, most guilds are planned around a central element, a single specimen that typically performs a number of functions. In permaculture this central figure is usually a fruit tree. In this example we'll use an apple tree. When planning your permaculture design, it is advisable to make getting your fruit trees into the ground one of the first tasks to complete, as they typically take several years to mature and provide you with a crop. Depending on the species, you will usually have to wait around five years to start harvesting a consistent crop of fruit. Once it is in the ground, however, it performs several functions in a guild. The apple tree can be a support for climbing plants; it offers protection to specimens that exist at lower levels (although the gardener may need to prune it occasionally to ensure that those lower down in the stack of the guild receive sufficient sunlight); it helps keep soil moisture levels

high; it provides habitat for birds which in turn can help to keep insect populations in balance; and it adds to the nutrient load of the soil as its leaves fall to the ground and are decomposed by microorganisms.

Incorporating plants into the apple tree guild that can serve as mulch can also ameliorate the soil. Such species can perform this function both when living as ground cover crops, and when slashed back and left to decompose where they fall, returning their nutrients to the soil and also helping to keep the topsoil well structured and so aiding water and air circulation within it. In an apple tree guild, comfrey, rhubarb and artichokes are common choices to perform this function. Rooters will also help improve the soil structure and raise its nutrient content, by bringing up elements from further down in the soil profile. Dandelions are a good choice for this role, as are yarrow and chicory. And, as with most guilds, including some specimens who act to fix nitrogen in the soil will help all the members of the guild by giving them access to good levels of this essential nutrient. Legumes such as clover, hairy vetch and

alfalfa work well in this regard in an apple tree guild and can provide forage for your livestock when cut back at the end of the growing season.

To keep your apple tree guild evolving over time and becoming self-sustaining, you need the plants within it to propagate. Attracting a variety of insect species to the guild is one of the best, and most energy efficient ways of doing this. Fennel, coriander and dill are good choices for increasing insect biodiversity in an apple tree guild.

When it comes to repelling damaging insects, however, nasturtiums are often incorporated into an apple tree guild, as they are particularly effective at keeping away insects that attack that type of fruit. In fact, many commercial orchards make use of this fact by planting nasturtiums among their apple trees to help protect their harvest. Nasturtiums also provide the secondary benefit of food for your kitchen, as their flowers are edible. They also add an aesthetically pleasing splash of colour to your guild.

Daffodils add colour too, but offer other benefits besides. For one thing they are very effective at deterring wild grazers such as deer and rabbits as these animals find them poisonous. Thus daffodils offer other members of the guild protection. They also help to suppress invasive species that would, given the chance, compete with the members of the guild for soil nutrients and moisture. Grasses and weeds – which have relatively shallow root systems – are suppressed due to the shallow, but more robust, rooting system of the daffodil. Alliums like garlic, chives and leeks are also valuable additions to the apple tree guild for the same reason, with the added bonus that because they keep a lot of their energy in a bulb below the surface of the soil, they go dormant over the summer, relying on the stores of nutrients and water in the bulb for sustenance rather than taking any from the surrounding soil. This benefits the other members of the guild, as there is less competition for these valuable elements at a time when, due to the higher temperatures of summer, they are likely to be scarcer. For a large, thirsty plant like a mature apple tree this can be vital. As such, when planning your guild, place a ring of alliums where the drip line of the mature apple tree will be.

Besides this array of plant species, the permaculture gardener can also promote connections between the apple tree guild and animals, by permitting occasional grazing by livestock for instance, or by providing habitat to attract beneficial wild species, both of which methods can help keep grasses, weeds and insect populations under control. An example of the latter would be adding logs and rocks to the location of the guild, as these create habitat niches for ground dwelling creatures. Positioning a pond nearby can also be of great benefit to a guild, attracting an even wider variety of insects and other animals to your property.

What is succesion planting?

Companion planting and guilds encourage and enhance the mutual benefits that plant species can gain from being connected to each other in a space, with the permaculture gardener harnessing those interrelations – and the ones the plants have with animals – to seek to maximize the yield from the plants. However, there is also a way that the gardener can seek such maximization through time as well as space.

Succession planting is designed to give you as much vegetable harvest from your garden beds as possible over the course of a growing season. While maximizing yield is the watchword for all permaculture projects, succession planting to create this abundance is particularly useful for gardeners with limited space. It can mean that you can harvest a variety of crops over time, and so avoid having a glut of vegetables when everything ripens simultaneously. Certain types of succession planting can also help to safeguard your property against crop failure. If you have a single planting of a single species, your whole yield is under threat if a soil pathogen, a blooming population of a pest insect, or an extreme weather event takes hold on your property or even in a single garden bed. Succession planting, by staggering the planting schedule, means you are at less risk of complete crop failure.

As mentioned, there are different strategies when it comes to succession planting. There are four main techniques that the permaculture gardener can use, but whichever one or combination of strategies you choose to use, there are factors that you need to consider before starting to plant, as these will influence the type of technique that is suitable for your property.

The first thing to consider is the length of the growing season. This is influenced by the general climate conditions that are prevalent in your geographical location – which in turn are modified by factors such as latitude, elevation, and orientation. If you are in a location that has short summers and long, cold winters, your choice of technique will likely differ from that of a gardener working in a place that enjoys a long summer and a mild winter. Climate factors may also be important to

get your free permaculture checklist now @
regenerative.com/book-checklist

Regenerative Leadership Institute
create a meaningful life doing what you love

consider in terms of the microclimates the areas you want to practice succession planting in are exposed to, which will be influenced by things such as the shade offered by buildings, fences or other plants, solar reflection and heat stored and emitted by certain elements of the site such as stones, walls and ponds.

These climatic – and microclimatic – factors will be the primary influence on the next important consideration for your succession-planting plan: the plants that you grow. Personal taste will also have an influence, but the required growing conditions of plant species will need to be taken into account. For instance, if you have short summers and the first frost of the year comes relatively early, you may well select plants that can withstand a cold snap, rather than those that suffer at the first sign of cold weather. You will need to look at expected maturation times for different species, so that you can estimate how long it will take from seed or seedling to harvestable crop – bearing in mind that some types of vegetable can actually be harvested before they are fully mature; think of "baby" peas, beets and carrots – they can give you an early harvest of edible crops as well as offering a distinctly different taste from their fully mature counterparts.

As a general rule to guide your plant selection, look for varieties that grow quickly, mature relatively fast and can be grown well in the individual climate conditions that you experience on your site. Research different cultivars within the same plant family as well to find those most suited to your needs and aims. In many instances, plants native to your area will be among the best options.

Four succession planting strategies

When it comes to actually planning your succession planting strategy, there are four primary techniques.

get your free permaculture checklist now @
regenerative.com/book-checklist

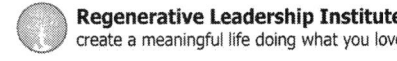
Regenerative Leadership Institute
create a meaningful life doing what you love

The first sees the same crop planted at successive intervals in the same bed. This will give you a staggered harvest over the growing season. Such a technique works best for quick-growing vegetables like salad greens, radishes and bush beans. Such species mature quickly, so you can plant seeds every few weeks and harvest appropriately. Remember that you will need to leave some space in your garden beds for the successive plantings – you aren't planting the next set of seeds once you have harvested the first; you plan so that several sets are in various stages of the maturation process. Lettuce for example, can be planted every two weeks. By the time you are putting in the fourth set, the first will be ready for harvest, with the subsequent sets maturing in order, and allowing you to plant your fifth set where the first has been harvested from.

The second strategy, conversely, only requires a single planting session. The succession aspect comes from the fact that you plant different species of vegetable together that have different maturation

get your free permaculture checklist now @
regenerative.com/book-checklist

Regenerative Leadership Institute
create a meaningful life doing what you love

times. This technique works best when you employ companion planting principles, so that crops growing together offer one another benefits and in doing so give the gardener the best chance of a robust harvest.

An example of this strategy is combining kale and lettuce in the same garden bed. They like complementary soil conditions, and the young lettuce benefits from having the hardier kale nearby to protect it. However, because lettuce matures a lot faster than the kale, it is ready to harvest before the kale gets too big to shade the lettuce out and inhibit growth. Once the lettuce has been harvested, the kale is able to utilize the extra room to grow into fully mature specimens for harvesting later in the season.

Similar to this technique is the third succession planting strategy, which is to plant the same type of plant, but combine different varieties that mature at different rates. This is useful if you have very specific soil or climate conditions that suit a certain type of crop, or if you need to grow a lot of one product for market. One vegetable commonly used in such a strategy is the tomato, which comes in a wide range of varieties. For instance, small cherry tomatoes ripen comparatively early in the season and continue producing fruit until early fall, while oxheart tomatoes, being that much larger, take longer to mature and offer their harvest from late summer to late fall. Again, this technique only requires a single planting session – the succession comes from the staggering of harvesting times.

The fourth strategy sees the permaculture gardener plant different types of vegetables one after the other, taking advantage of the different growing conditions throughout the season. For example, you could first plant a crop that favors the cooler climate of spring – such as cabbage or peas – and then follow it with a species that needs more exposure to the sunshine and temperatures that come with high summer in order to mature – such as eggplant.

Succession planting tips

Whichever strategy you choose to employ, there are a few tips that can help make the process run smoothly and ensure the best results. For instance, it is a good idea to keep a record of your succession planting for each bed in which you employ it. Either in a spreadsheet on your computer or in a notebook, note down the species that you plant, when you plant them, any mulch or soil modifications your utilize, and when you expect to get a viable harvest from them. It can also be beneficial to write down pertinent information that will impact upon your growing strategy, such as the date of the first frost. As you harvest crops, make some notes on the abundance and quality of the produce you are getting for your kitchen, and anything you notice about the condition of the plants. This will help you make any necessary adjustments to planting strategies for the following year. Keeping such a record will also help you with the rotation of crops through different garden beds. It is advisable to not grow the same species of vegetable in the same location year after year, as this will affect the chances of securing reliable bountiful yields. We will explore rotation in more detail in the following section.

Such a record will also make it easier to plan in advance for the following year's succession planting effort. It will enable you to make sure you have enough of the right seeds to get planting at the optimum moment on the calendar. You may also – particularly if you live in a location that has a short growing season – wish to start your seeds off indoors or in a greenhouse or cold frame. This can give you a head start on the growing season, allowing your seeds to germinate while outside it is still too cold for them to do so, and then planting out seedlings rather than seeds.

As you progress through your succession-planting plan, especially the first technique, it can be a good strategy to add organic compost with each new planting. This will ensure that each planting gets all the nutrients it needs to keep yield at its maximum. And speaking of maximizing yield, don't feel as though you have to wait for every plant to mature before you can replace the crop with next one. Inevitably, some specimens will do better than others, and you don't want to be lingering over one or two plants when the rest of the bed is not being productive. After the lion's share of the crop has been harvested and production of that species declines, remove the plants – remembering to add them to the compost pile so that their energy does not go to waste – and commence with the next planting.

Rotation planting

This form of succession planting, with different plant species following one another in the same location can also be extended out to apply not only across a single growing season, but over successive years. You can think of it a little like what farmers call crop rotation, and it

has many of the same benefits as that larger scale form. In the past, farmers routinely used crop rotation practices to help preserve the productivity of their crops. In the modern industrial age of monocultures supported by large inputs of inorganic fertilizers and pesticides, it is not so widespread, but it is a common practice on organic farms, as it is one of the best methods of keeping soil diseases and pests under control without the need for damaging chemical biocides.

So organic farmers rotate crops through different fields so that the same species of crop is not planted in the same patch of earth over successive growing seasons. This helps mitigate the influence of soil pathogens and destructive microorganisms, which typically build up when a single crop is continuously grown in the same field. Many pathogens and harmful bacteria primarily target a certain species or family of plants. If the same crop is grown in the same area of soil continually or at least over several growing seasons, it allows the damaging elements the time to build up and "get used to" the conditions

(such as the soil structure and nutritional load demanded by the plant to grow well). This can, in the worst instances, eventually lead to crop failure. By rotating the crops, with different families following one another in the same field, these harmful microorganisms are kept in check. The same goes for potentially damaging pest insect populations. Many pests favor particular species or families of vegetable, grain or fruit, and by rotating crops the farmer disrupts their foraging patterns, so protecting his crops.

Farmers also use crop rotation in order to utilize the physical properties of different species to make the field suitable for a different crop to follow in, such as using a deep-rooting species to break up and improve the soil structure for a shallower rooting crop to follow, or by using one species to increase the levels of a soil nutrient that the succeeding one particularly needs in order to grow to its potential – for instance, by following a leguminous vegetable that boosts the nitrogen levels in the soil with a species that requires high levels of that chemical element in order to set an abundant crop. Both these benefits help to maximize the yield of the crops, by protecting them from damage and by giving them the best conditions in which to grow.

You can institute a similar form of crop rotation on your permaculture property; even if rather than fields you are simply growing in garden beds. You will reap the same benefits of suppressing pests and improving soil conditions for different species. Let's take a look at a common vegetable crop rotation through four beds that can be easily instituted on almost any permaculture property. You use four different families of plants that require different conditions to thrive in, and rotate them through each of four beds over four years, changing their position annually after harvesting. Four years is generally regarded – not only on small permaculture designs but also on the agricultural scale – as the minimum time that should be allowed to elapse before the same crop is planted in an area of ground that it has been cultivated in before. This prevents excessive depletion of any essential soil nutrients and so gives the best chance of maximum yield. Of course, such a system may well need adapting depending on the unique conditions of your site – and you would choose species within each group that you particularly want to grow and eat – but the general reasons for the pattern and this particular rotation are a good guide for your planting plan.

Within each of the four groups of vegetable plants in this example, the individual specimens have similar growing needs and so do well when planted in the same bed. They will all benefit from the conditions put in place by the preceding crop, and will have similar interrelationships with insects in terms of pollination and pest protection.

The first group is the Brassicas - which includes plants such as cauliflower, kale, broccoli and Brussels sprouts – alongside other leafy green vegetables such as spinach and lettuce. All these plant species are heavy feeders of soil nutrients.

The second group comprises leguminous vegetables, such as okra, peas, beans and peanuts. As we've seen, these species have a symbiotic relationship with certain bacteria meaning that they "fix" nitrogen in the soil, boosting its levels more than most other plants. Following the first group with these legumes helps to replenish the soil of the nutrients that the heavy feeders in group one have used. Farmers will often use fields of alfalfa or clover as their leguminous crop. In both cases – agricultural and home gardening – the plants are slashed and left to rot on the garden bed after the crop has been harvested. This further boosts the nutritional content of the soil.

The legumes are therefore followed by a group of plants that need a nutrient-rich soil in order to grow robustly. Thus group three is made up of members of the allium family. Plants such as chives, leeks onions, shallots and garlic will do well in the rich topsoil left behind by the legumes

The fourth group comprises rooting and fruiting vegetables. Beets, carrots, potatoes, tomatoes and capsicums could all be included in this group, and as they grow they send down deep roots to access nutrients and soil moisture, improving the structure of the soil profile as they do. This helps to provide the loose soil structure that the Brassicas and leafy green vegetables prefer when they follow such species in the rotational sequence.

So, for these four groups the succession of the rotation would see each following their numerical predecessor into the same bed. Imagine four beds at each primary point of a compass, with the first bed at north, the second on the point of east, and so on round the system. In the first year the Brassicas are in bed one, the rooting vegetables will be placed in bed two, the alliums will be planted in bed three and the legumes will be in the fourth bed. Then, in the second year, the gardener would rotate the crops clockwise through the beds, moving each on one bed. This means that bed one is now

host to legumes, the Brassicas now take up residence in bed two, the rooting vegetables have bed three to themselves, and the alliums make themselves at home in bed four. For each of the next two years, this rotation is repeated, so that by the fifth year, the plant groups are back in their initial beds.

Such a rotation should ensure that you give your crops the best chance of growing healthily and providing you with an abundant harvest. Combining with other permaculture techniques – such as mulching, adding organic compost and using windbreaks to protect plants from the elements – where necessary should mean that you have a rotational system that can be continued for as many seasons as you wish. However, at some point you may want to replenish the nutritional content of a bed even more than the rotation allows. This is likely to be necessary as well if you are looking to rehabilitate damaged soil for your permaculture property. In such cases, interrupting the rotational cycle to plant a cover crop in the bed – comfrey is a good choice, as is clover

– that will improve the nutrient levels when growing and can be slashed and left to further augment the soil through decomposition can be a good strategy. Farmers sometimes use this method on their fields, but may also utilize the technique of leaving a field fallow for a year. This means simply leaving the field untouched and uncultivated. It allows nature to colonize the area, typically with grasses and weed species that will perform similar augmentations to the soil as a deliberately sown cover crop. You could do the same with your garden beds, if you wish, but whereas farmers will often plough or use livestock grazing to remove the grasses when they wish to recommence planting, the permaculture gardener will probably need to use some form of mulching – such as solarising black plastic – to rid the bed of the grasses and weeds and make it ready for food crops again.

Made in the USA
Coppell, TX
31 May 2021